RUNNING FOR CLOCKS AND DESSERT SPOONS

Sporting Lives

Edited
by
Ian Clayton

Speaking From Experience

Yorkshire Art Circus
1988

CONTENTS

ACKNOWLEDGEMENTS

The following people have helped to make this project possible:

Rachel Adam
Jill Brown
Wayne Clarida
Olive Fowler
Brian Lewis
Heather Parkinson
David Prudhoe
Rachel Van Riel
Joan Thornton

DEDICATION

All the contributors to this book provided fascinating stories and real insight into *Sporting Lives*. Sadly Ted Fletcher and Alice Brear died before publication. We wish to dedicate the book to their memories.

Published by Yorkshire Art Circus
13-15 Sagar Street, Castleford, West Yorkshire, WF10 1AG

Typeset by Print Assist, Castleford.
Printed by F.M. Reprographic, Ravensthorpe, Dewsbury.

INTRODUCTION

This is a book by and about sportsmen and sportswomen; about enthusiasts for sport rather than champions. Some chose to give a potted history of their favourite sport, others talked about enjoyment through their involvement. This is not a season by season list of who won what, or who finished second and third. Neither does it deal with statistics but aims to present a glimpse into the everyday aspects of sporting life.

Sport for All once a popular slogan – is still possible

SWIMMING

"Never eat Pizza before an attempt on the Channel"

Yvonne Carter started swimming at the age of eight – "Mum thought it necessary in case of accident." She became a club champion by the age of ten, went on to represent Great Britain and during August 1986 achieved her ambition of swimming the English channel.

I suppose I took, as they say, to water like a duck. I swam both a width and a length on only my second lesson. I learned the basic stroke techniques with the Wakefield Kingfishers Club with whom I stayed for two years. At the age of ten I joined Dewsbury swimming club, which is a competitive club and it was here I met Eileen Fenton, the club coach, who later became my Channel swim coach and was herself a former Channel swimmer.

Even though I wanted to compete, I hadn't bargained for the gruelling sessions Miss Fenton put me through. Up at five-thirty every day from Monday to Friday, in the water for six o'clock and out again at eight in time for school. Then after school it was back to the pool for another two hours. Saturday was either a rest day or competition day followed by more training on Sunday.

I wasn't much good at short distances but I proved myself at eight hundred metres and above. When I was only eleven, I competed with sixteen and seventeen year olds in the local galas. The club also went in for the big competitions, like the North Eastern Counties and the National Open Age.

At the age of thirteen, Miss Fenton asked me if I would like to try my hand at long distance swimming. I spent the whole winter looking through the *Swimming Times*, a magazine of swimming news. Then during the spring of 1981 I received my baptism in cold water, swimming in the Sparth reservoir at the other side of

Huddersfield, where the water runs straight off the Pennines. I managed half a mile the first time and stayed in longer and longer on each occasion. Gradually I conquered my fear of being unable to see the bottom and learned to cope with the cold. My personality seemed to change in the water, I felt a sense of power I didn't seem to have on dry land – and more confidence every time.

The long distance swimming season starts in May and my first event was on Langold Lake near Worksop. This was a two mile event which, to everyone's surprise and especially my own, I won. I went on to swim in about eighteen more races that year and set new records in twelve of them. This was despite reservations most other swimmers had about my height.

My younger brother Clive used to travel with us to the competitions. More often than not he wanted to go home before the swim even started, but then one day he saw a group of canoeists assisting at a match. He decided he'd have a go and has never looked back. Today he is one of the most sought after canoeists in the British Long Distance Swimming Association. He has canoed on Lake Windermere, Bala in Wales and the difficult Torbay swim. He was the first Yorkshire canoeist to pass the Escort Award and when he doesn't canoe for me, he is always snapped up by other swimmers.

In 1982 a new event, the *Champion of Champions* was started. It was the hardest event ever for juniors like myself, and for the seniors, it was used as a international trial. It comprises three events in the same day – six miles in the morning, three after lunch and then one in the evening. The winner is the one with the fastest time when the three have been added together. I was selected to represent Britain in this event and swam in Spain where I finished third and Belgium where I came second.

The Spanish trip sticks in mind because of the huge amount of frogs in the river. The English team had frog races with them when they should have been training! Yugoslavia was one of the best trips, not just for the sun and sea, but for the great friends I made there which has been one of the best things to come out of my enjoyment for sport.

My training for the Channel swim started in earnest at the end of the summer season. Being fit enough however was only one of my worries. The finances were another headache. We needed money; for the fishing boat which would accompany me, membership fees for the Channel Swim Association (which everyone planning the swim has to join), training fees, travelling costs and accomodation fees. We formed a committee consisting of family and friends and held coffee mornings, raffles and sponsored swims. With donations from local businesses, we managed to raise £2450 which more than covered the costs.

I trained twice a day with Miss Fenton; four hours at Sun Lane baths, Wakefield and on Sundays at Normanton Baths. The old training sessions were nothing compared to these times of agony.

As soon as the weather permitted, Miss Fenton decided I should go outdoors and get used to the cold water — *freezing* would be a better term. Now we trained for two hours inside and two outdoors. At first we had difficulty getting permission to train in the local lakes. For a time I ignored *No Swimming* notices at the Mill Field Lagoon at Wakefield and always tried to stay in the middle so as not to annoy anglers on the banks. Although several of the fishermen got used to seeing me after a while and became interested in what I was doing.

Finally, permission granted, I trained at Wintersett Reservoir. I have never seen a lake with water as clear as that. I used to look for fish, sometimes I saw trout but it was mostly tiddlers.

As the time grew nearer, I built up my training to four hours inside and six hours outdoors to improve stamina and resistance to cold. On Sundays I did eight hours — four in the morning and four at night — to get used to night swimming. It's amazing how many odd sounds and smells there are when you're plodding up and down a lake at midnight.

Eventually the time came to go to Folkestone. Three of us went, Miss Fenton and my mum accompanying me. I had to get used to sea swimming and swam in the harbour. I also needed to overcome my fear of jellyfish. I hoped I would never be faced with a ten foot monster like the Portuguese-man-of-war I had once seen off

Torbay. And a few weeks before I went to Folkestone, I had seen a television programme about the Australian Box jellyfish, which can easily kill a person. Hardly confidence building and even today I shudder to think about jellyfish.

An Egyptian team of disabled swimmers were training for a two way relay swim so we decided to train with them. They set off the night before me and I heard they were successful in their attempt, amid much confusion. Their pilot boat only realised they were swimming both ways when they turned round on reaching France.

On the actual day of the swim I had two hours notice that *today was the day*. I had been held up by the remnants of *Hurricane Charlie*, but now my chance came on the last of the neap or slack tides.

The day was a scorcher, I couldn't eat breakfast, all I wanted to do was *grease up* and keep warm. I greased myself with lanolin, rubbing it well into the vital areas; kidneys and liver, my neck to prevent sunburn, shoulders to stop the costume rubbing and round my ankles, knees and groin.

On the boat was Mr Reid the pilot, two crewmen, Miss Fenton and an official Channel Swimming Association observer. The observer keeps a log of when the swimmer feeds and ensures that everything is done in accordance with the rules. There has to be no contact whatsoever even when the food is passed – it has to be taken cleanly out of the hand.

For the first two hours I couldn't stop laughing; the sun was shining, the water warm and there were no jellyfish. I could not believe my luck. Then half-way things went a bit wrong. I was sick twice – a combination of salt water and the previous night's pizza. Being sick slowed me down. Till then I was in sight of the British record of eight hours fifty six minutes, held by Wendy Brook. The world record is held by a Dutch woman called Irene Van der Laan.

The landing at Cap Gris Nez in France was a bit of an anti-climax. It was dark and there was nobody there; just loads of seaweed and barnacle covered rocks. Thirty metres from the shore the boat stopped. I was terrified that it had broken down but the two crewmen got into an inflatable dinghy and went the last few yards with me. I touched the main body of rocks and heard Miss Fenton cheer. Then I climbed into the dinghy and thanked God it was over. Arriving back at the fishing boat I just could not climb in no matter how hard I tried. At last I made it, but when the pilot let go of my arms, my legs, like jelly gave way and I sat on the deck in an undignified heap.

By then all the family had arrived in Folkestone and as soon as they heard the news went straight into a pub to celebrate.

I didn't fully realised my achievement till I was presented with trophies for being the fastest Briton and the fastest woman that year and entertained to dinner by the Channel Swim Association.

However, the real enjoyment and satisfaction comes from the excellent backing I have had from my parents and friends and a brilliant coach in Miss Fenton.

Yvonne Carter with Egyptian Relay Team of disabled swimmers at Folkstone

Billy Williams, Olympian studio pose

BOXING

"Some couldn't bost a grape."

Harold Coule first 'put the gloves on' as a nine year old. He retired twenty years and over one hundred fights later after a fight in Westmoreland. He was never knocked out once in his lengthy career.

Well it all started up at Rovers' field. We'd pinched into the stand to watch the boxing they'd organised during a pit strike. This lad was stripped and ready to box and his opponent hadn't turned up. My mates got on to me to have a go at him. I didn't take much egging on and ended up in the ring with him – barefoot, stripped and ready. I must have put a good show up because the crowd cheered me all way through and then rolled me up with money till I didn't know what to do with it. I daren't tell my father and ended up leaving it on the table hoping he'd think it was a gas rebate or something, but there was more money on the table than we'd ever put in the gas.

Anyhow after that I carried on fighting. I was George Street School's representative and won the Schoolboy's Championship at Bradford. I turned professional after school and fought all over the place. I beat 'Kid Chocolate', a black kid at Otley, knocked him out in six. Billy Johnson of Manchester, I won him at Barnsley and Loll Nutbrown, Sheffield champion, I beat him at Castle in Pontefract.

During the 1926 strike they promoted boxing at the Miners Welfare. We kept kids with three meals a day through boxing, we even gave clothes away at the front door.

I was fighting at nine stone nine at that time, that's lightweight, but I'd get in with the welters if I could get a fight with one.

Professor Marks of Leeds heard about me and took me under his wing as manager-come-trainer. He had a gym near the National

Sports Club in Leeds. They all went there. I remember Al Foreman coming. He held the English belt at the time and was down to fight Don Volante of Liverpool. So Marks says to me, "Get on wi 'im Harold."

They put twenty-eight ounce gloves on me so I couldn't hurt him. You see, with gloves like that you can't hit as fast and your arms get tired quick. I got stuck in though and knocked nobs off him, I tried to put him out. He didn't want to know after two rounds.

He was a decent chap was Professor Marks, but the two who showed me how to carry on and learned me the game were a couple of miners who come up from Abergevenny or somewhere. One of them fought as Johnny Cole during the first war and his mate was a little stiff bloke called Ikey Jones. Only a little bloke but he'd a grand physique. He could waff a towel for fifteen rounds, you knew you'd got some air when he was waffing. You see, them halls used to fill up with cig smoke till it burned your lungs. You needed a good waffer between rounds.

Them two told me more than any. They knew how to put bandages on with layers of plaster in between and when to use grease and vaseline and what have you. When there was any betting on a fight they'd be whispering, "Tha's favourite Harold, but don't put him out straight away, let him shine a bit first and get money up."

Then you'd go into the ring and fair hear the clink of money changing hands.

I fought at Sheffield in 1930, it was open air fighting there at Hyde Park. 'Nipper' Moore and 'Pongo' Jenkinson were on the same bill and I was matched against Arly Hollingsworth and fought him to a draw. A couple of weeks after, Arly went to France and fought Emil 'Spider' Pladner, the World Flyweight Champion, and only just lost on points.

Another time I went to Bradford on the Monday and fought top of the bill. I beat the Midlands champion. I fought again on the Friday at Blackpool Tower Circus against an American that was touring over here. When I got back on the Saturday night there was a train waiting to take me to Leeds to fight Sunday morning on a bill promoted by Albert Hislop, a Featherstone man. Jimmy Learoyd was down to fight Tommy Marron the Northern Champion, but he couldn't get so they sent for me. Well, from me landing at home on Saturday night, they filled seven bus loads for the trip to Leeds on Sunday morning. When the referee gave a draw they nearly broke the place down, they'd to fetch the bobbies in the end.

That wasn't unusual though in them days, bobbies often turned up. Spectators took their boxing seriously, specially if there was any money on. They'd stand for no califudging in the ring. They knew some boxers were good lads and that others *couldn't bost a grape.*

I always put up a good show, but I knew when I'd had enough. I retired in 1941 and they had a collection for me. I told them I didn't want money, so they bought me a cup engraved with all my stuff.

Billy Williams with a left upper-cut in a fight in Featherstone square

"The Methodist Preacher and the little black devil"

Perhaps the greatest of all local boxers however was Billy Williams, an all round sportsman of considerable ability. Apart from boxing, he maintained a link with Featherstone Rovers for almost seventy years. Miss Elsie Williams, Billy's daughter tells of his exploits.

Dad started boxing in 1913 just after his seventeenth birthday. In that same year, he knocked his opponent out to win the Yorkshire Middleweight Cup and just after that won the North of England championship.

A lot of people wouldn't know that boxing took place at the Hippodrome Picture House in Featherstone, but in 1916 Dad was top of the bill there. He fought 'Young' Rice of Newcastle who'd already won over fifty contests, and beat him easily. It used to be ls 6d to go in, or you could have a ringside seat for 3s 6d and there were at least half a dozen fights. A popular attraction at the time were The Brothers Lee who went as 'The Fighting Midgets' – they were circus dwarfs.

After beating 'Young' Rice, Billy Bullock and Private Holmes, the army champion from Pontefract barracks; the newspapers reported that father was rapidly running out of opponents and that he had *repeatedly challenged any pitman at eleven stone without response.* Finally, Joe Varley the well known Castleford fighter agreed to a match and a big purse of £75 was put up for a fight at Pontefract Town Hall in 1916. It was a big bill with two Hague's from Mexborough, (relatives of the famous 'Iron' Hague, world title challenger) boxing in supporting bouts. Father overcame Varley with superior fitness in a hard fight which went the full twelve rounds – Dad winning on points. The papers said, *Varley was severely punished, but held on grimly till the end.*

After this, Dad was due to fight in Leeds, but after being instructed to *take a dive*, he promptly refused and declared his intention to get out of the fighting game. Thus his record of twenty wins in twenty fights remains unchanged.

However, there may have been more to his decision to quit than just his dissatisfaction with these cheaters. A travelling evangelist had spoken to Father on several occasions and finally persuaded him to become involved in the church. He became a devoted methodist and in 1921 became a lay preacher at Purston Methodist Church. His devotion to church work was only equalled by his love of sport.

Apart from boxing he was a wrestling champion, a rugby forward with Featherstone Rovers, a fine swimmer and a medallist at diving. He also coached Featherstone Rovers, had a physiotherapy practice and was head of physiotherapy at Pontefract Infirmary. In later life, he pursued another interest. He wrote poetry and had five books published, giving the proceeds to the Church.

Billy's brother Jimmy Williams was also a great sportsman. He was the first man to score for Featherstone Rovers in a senior match when he dropped a goal at Bradford in the first minute. He was also coach of the now forgotten Newcastle Rugby Club and during the summer was wicket keeper for Hemsworth in the Yorkshire Council League. A very tigerish fellow – folk round here nicknamed him *The Little Black Devil*.

ATHLETICS

"Shall we finish together?"

Gerald Brookman started running at Normanton Grammar School in the early 1950's and eventually joined the now defunct Pontefract and Castleford Athletic Club. Later he ran for Wakefield Harriers in the half mile and mile handicaps in locally organised competitions. Running and sprinting in particular, has always been popular amongst sports folk of this area. The naked imitators of Olympians who streaked down Pontefract Road in the last century and Rugby players like Charlie Dutton, Ernest Jordan, 'Buff' Lord and Walt Schofield who run for money in the Sheffield Handicap belong to this great tradition.

Nobody made much money out of those handicap races – almost everybody was amateur and the top prize money for amateurs was set at seven guineas win, four guineas second and two guineas for third place. Then there were other prizes like clocks and canteens of cutlery – we must have had clocks all over our house, I lost count how many. Professionalism started at seven guineas, but the bread and butter races were the handicaps. Even the top runners like Derek Ibbotson and perhaps even Bannister, started off running for knives, forks and spoons.

In those times track events were organised by sports organisations attached to works, like Lumbs Glass of Castleford, ICI at Huddersfield, the Yorkshire Copperworks or the collieries at Galas. Although most of the runners represented clubs, it was more of an individual's race because of the handicapping system. Local town sports days at Altofts and Normanton might have been off scratch, that is to say everybody set off together, but as a rule, most races were run under the handicap system. In mile races you might get everything – from scratch to a bloke starting two hundred yards in front. The official handicapper used to visit most of the sports events. If you won a race, you'd go to him and he'd make an instant decision as to whether or not your handicap needed reducing. Everybody looked in the Sunday papers then to see the handicapper's tables.

I remember a funny story about the handicap start at a half mile race I'd entered. A young lad from Featherstone came across as we were lining up and asked "How do I go on with this staggered start? I've never been in one before."

I told him that first of all the starter would blow his whistle and then pause a second or two before firing his pistol. So if he wanted to get a clear start, set off when he heard the whistle – you see with up to forty starting in different places the umpires couldn't keep an eye on everybody. I also warned him that at the gun everybody would run like mad to get a place, then slow down to a more even pace before sprinting to the line.

After the race the lad came up very disappointed at having finished last. "I did everything tha told me," he complained. "But while I waited for them to slow down to that even pace – they all went past me!"

At Lumb's Sports Day, they had what they call a *Mile Medley*. Two men ran 220 yards, one ran a quarter mile leg and then passed the baton to the fourth man who ran the final half mile. There were about nine teams in this race and I was running for Pontefract in the last leg. We weighed up the opposition and decided that the Halifax Club were obvious favourites – they had all the top men, including the County Champion at half mile. We were in with a shout for second place, but the prize was a box of dessert spoons and forks which none of us wanted. Third prize though was a watch, so that's what we decided to go for.

Over the first three legs, the race went true to form, Halifax duly shot off into the lead with us nicely placed at the front of the chasing pack. Anyhow, comes the last leg and I find myself in second place, thinking about the watch I started to slow down. Nobody passed me, so I slowed down some more and still nobody passed me, the line was now fast approaching and still nobody made a move. I dared not slow down anymore and had to go through the tape in second place to win the spoons. Everybody obviously had the same idea as us, preferring a watch apiece to a box of spoons.

I suppose folk start running for a variety of reasons. When I cast my mind back, I think my main inspiration was an old chap who lived next door when I was a kid. I'd always been a decent runner but never took it seriously. This old neighbour used to sit on his step many an hour telling me about the old time professionals in this area. They rarely trained but possessed real raw talent. They'd take eggs and sherry before a race, that sort of thing.

When I went to Normanton Grammar School they were short for a cross country race so I decided to enter to make the numbers up. Near the finish I was running alongside a much older lad, he turned round and said, "Shall we finish together?."

I must have had a fine disregard for the Olympian spirit, because in reply I set off sprinting. "No....I'm going," I shouted, and beat him in the dash to the line. After that I broke the school mile record which had stood for thirteen years. The Headmaster mentioned it in my testimonial.

After leaving school, I joined Pontefract and Castleford Athletic Club. It has to be said that the organisation was not very good. We had very little coaching, rarely trained with each other and only came together on the day of the meeting. I did most of my training alone, running endless laps of the local cricket fields in all weathers. Then eventually I got a coach, Mr Colin Clarkson, a school teacher. He introduced me to *Interval Running* – that was running a sixty second quarter mile (or four-forty as we called it then), then walking a quarter, before running again ....and so on. Pretty spartan training techniques but I suppose it goes back to what my old neighbour told me – if you've got the raw talent you don't need much else.

There were still a few of the old fashioned type of runners knocking about at that time as well. I remember Jim Cadman, a six foot two inch coal miner from Pontefract, a quarter mile champion – all arms and legs. He'd do a Saturday morning shift down the pit, come up and elbow his opponents out of the way to win a race the same afternoon. Like a lot of runners, Jim went in for what might be termed novelty events like coal carrying races and such, for money. At other times, they might have a mixed meeting of bicyle races and ordinary running.

When clubs started to get more organised and competitive the handicaps went into decline and the days of fun running were numbered. It became fashionable to represent your club rather than run for individual gain. Clubs got professional; flashy vests and kits, new colours and what have you. It spoiled a lot of the fun for the moderate runners. Obviously, in some ways it was a good thing, because better organisation led to better facilities and then to better coaching and undoubtedly, to a higher standard of running. At the same time though a big gap was left by the decline in the handicap races and prize galas which has only just recently been filled again by people's marathons, fun runs and jogging.

On the positive side, it shows what can be done by improving facilities. Clubs like Wakefield Harriers who are big enough and well enough organised to survive, attract scores of youngsters to training sessions. Women's athletics in this area was given a real boost when Dorothy Hyman, the international runner from Cudworth, formed the Dorothy Hyman Track Club and the local council backed her by building the Hyman Stadium with an all-weather, tartan track.

There is a lot to be said for good facilities. Enthusiastic youngsters leaving school need raw talent developing. Good facilities make moderate runners into good athletes and there is nothing worse than talent wasted. One thing I remember from my training was the soul destroying feature of it. They talk about the loneliness of the long distance runners – the distance doesn't matter. The loneliness of training for any event is the hardest part. Managing a race every Saturday during the summer made it worth it though, and then there were the cross country races in the winter.

When I first started you thought you were a proper athlete if you had a track suit, but our coach always used to say, "Don't worry about a bloke in a new track suit and spikes, worry about one with battered spikes, scruffy blue bottoms and a dirty old maroon top – he's a champion.'' He said it at one meeting and as though to prove it, Nicholls, the six mile champ from Sheffield, trotted across behind him wearing scuffed spikes, scruffy blue bottoms and an old maroon top!

Featherstone Swimming and Diving Club

THEY'RE THE 'DOLLY ROCKERS', all set for a training session at Purston Park. Left to right, this attractive new soccer line-up is: Margaret Ashton (captain), Jane Summers, Jean Townend, Gillian Millard, Ann Durham, Janet Tennant, Janet Davis, Janice Roberts, Janet Baxter, Lynne Plant and Christine Carter.

WOMEN'S SOCCER

"Boots Two Sizes Too Big"

Women's soccer rose in popularity during the 1960's. There were several very good teams in the North of England, one of the best locally was the 'Dolly Rockers'. They had their beginnings in the late sixties and had their share of success, but disbanded during the mid seventies due to lack of backing. Maggie Ashton captained the 'Dolly Rockers' throughout their short history and was instrumental in the club's success.

You might wonder, why the name 'Dolly Rockers'? Well I suppose we were all tomboys really. When we hung about in the Hideaway Cafe we would pass the crash helmet round for donations for the juke box. A lot of the lads had motorbikes, some of them had scooters, you know the old Mods and Rockers thing. I suppose we favoured the Rockers, hence 'Dolly Rockers'.

It all started with this gang of lasses who used to meet in the Hideaway, and other girls who came to the disco at Featherstone Rovers Social Club on Friday nights. One night at the disco some girls from Normanton challenged us Featherstone lasses to get a team up and play a game at Purston Park.

We borrowed strip from the Miners Welfare Club and asked brothers and their mates for boots. I remember we'd to pull the laces as tight as we could because the boots fit us like flippers. We grabbed a lad and persuaded him to referee, put jumpers down for goalposts and ended up winning ten – nil.

It snowballed from there. We started training regularly. My dad acted as manager, my sister as secretary and our front room became Headquarters. We'd still to go knocking doors for boots of course, but with parents' involvement we got quite well organised.

It must have been 1969 or 1970 when we applied to join the West

Yorkshire League. By this time, through parents holding coffee mornings, sponsored walks and raffles, we raised enough money to buy our own strip. We chose green and white colours styled like Hibernian, the top Scottish club. We thought theirs were the best looking shirts at the time.

Of course involvement in the League meant a proper official approach to the game. We borrowed goal nets from Birshall's A.F.C., paid registration and subscription fees for all our players and obtained insurance. We received copies of the League's rules and regulations and started training in earnest.

By this time we had two trainers, Les and Frank from South Elmsall. The team din't need much training though, most of them were just out of school and fit enough. After a while we got Stuart as Trainer. He was a P.E. teacher and by hell did he put us through it? Press ups, squats, pull ups on the wall bars. He used to say, "Don't think you're getting special treatement because you're lasses, you'll do the same as the men." And we did. We'd finish training completely knackered. My Dad used to pick us up in his car after the sessions and ten of us used to pile in. Imagine that, ten of us in a bloody Hillman Imp and one of them a six foot tall goalie.

The girls came from all walks of life; sewing factories, sweet factories, secretaries and schoolgirls (some as young as fourteen,) and we'd one who was training in the legal profession to be a lawyer or something. They came from all over the place as well; Kinsley, Featherstone, Normanton, Altofts, Pontefract and Hemsworth.

One of the main problems was getting folk to take us seriously. The local press helped us a bit by publicising our efforts but they didn't seem to recognise our commitment. I think at first they wanted to make a joke of it all, doing light hearted pieces – but evenually we convinced them of our keenness. It was the same with a lot of the men who turned up at our games. First they came to laugh and poke fun, but when they saw the tackling and the goal scoring they were shocked. We wiped the smiles off a few faces.

We used to say, "We're as good as the lads because we've bin brought up wi'em!" After a while, they came along to support us and in big games we often attracted two or three hundred fans.

In the West Yorkshire League we played teams from all over the county. There weren't many women's clubs so it meant travelling a lot and we played at Leeds, Doncaster and at Haworth against 'The Brontes'. We couldn't always get a pitch at our local park because the Council preferred to give them to the men's teams first, so a lot of the time we had to play away anyhow.

The 'Fleece Fillies' of Ossett were the best team in Yorkshire, but they never liked playing us because we always gave them a hard game. They always put on a good spread after the match though – plenty to eat and plenty to drink. We'd get back to the coach singing at the top of our voices, then back at my mam's house we'd race each other for use of the lavatory and be queueing down the stairs.

The 'Fillies' had some good players, one or two internationals among them I think. One of them, only thirteen years old, was called Pat Firth and she played all over. At school, she captained the boys team and had medals for playing in Belgium. She played centre-forward and scored nearly a hundred goals in one year for the 'Fleece Fillies'. She was once on Yorkshire Television, on *Calendar* and mentioned that the Featherstone 'Dolly Rockers' were their most feared opponents.

A lot of the best women's soccer clubs came from Cheshire, the best was probably 'Foden Ladies'. We went to Manchester to see them play Scotland at Belle Vue Stadium. Hughie Green from *Opportunity Knocks* and Billy Butlin organised a ladies football competition and all the early rounds were played at holiday camps. 'Foden Ladies' representing England won two – nil.

One time the wireless programme *Down Your Way* featured Featherstone, and Franklin Engellmann spent a whole day here interviewing folk. He was a grand big bloke, well over six foot and a proper gentleman. He interviewed the 'Dolly Rockers' and really enjoyed himself. He spoke to myself, Lynn and Janet our ace goal scorer – we used to call her 'Wheels'. We'd nicknames for most of the players; there was 'Tank', 'Knees', 'Biddy' and 'Trolley'.

After a few seasons in the league we began to fade a bit. In fact women's football on the whole went into a decline. There were various reasons; the League set up wasn't exactly stable, teams came and went just as quickly, a lot of clubs had difficulty fielding their best sides, quite a few of the women were married with kids, and others had husbands working shifts. It didn't deter some mind, I've known some of the lasses bring their young ones in the pram and park them on the touch line while they played.

It wasn't that we lacked commitment we'd probably more go in us than the men. In fact once, when two men's games on adjacent pitches were abandoned due to bad weather conditions, we carried on. Another time we played in blinding snow and freezing cold, our laces froze hard to our boots and we couldn't undo them. Men watching were shouting that our game should be called off – but we still played on. So you see the enthusiasm was there all right but we didn't get chance to become established.

In the 'Dolly Rockers' case the main draw back was money. We had so many outgoings what with referees fees, ground fees, bus hire, league expenses and insurance, we just couldn't afford to do it. You can't survive forever on the proceeds of shilling coffee evenings. The other thing was lack of backing from local businesses, apart from Mr Price's sports shop in Pontefract, we got nothing, unlike a lot of the men's clubs. And because the Council couldn't promise us a pitch on a regular basis it meant us having to find money to travel away all the time. We also had our share of injuries – pulled muscles and sprained ankles meant time off work, which didn't go down too well. In the end, we dropped out of the League and decided to concentrate on friendlies and games for charity.

Once we played Featherstone Rovers at soccer in the local gala. We also played games in aid of cancer research and one match in aid of kidney research to help Mr Robinson, the Castleford specialist. A combination of 'Dolly Rockers' and Castleford nurses played Castleford police in that one. We also took on the teachers from Carleton School, Pontefract and gave them a rough time. The local newspapers said that we beat them at soccer and at Rugby as well!

One of the best laughs was at Rotherham Gala, after the match we had a wheelbarrow race. Chris tipped Jane out of the barrow right in front of the local vicarage – the air turned blue with bad language till Jane looked around and saw the local vicar standing right behind. Another time we were at Ossett, we came off the field caked in mud, stripped off for the bath and noticed the referee sat there. "It's alreet lasses," he shouts, "I can't see owt we'art me glasses." Then there was the occasion we played some women from Knottingley who came trotting on in bloody curlers and hairnets!

In a way it was a shame that we ended up just playing novelty games after such a promising start. But we certainly had some great times; crowding into my mam's front room for meetings while she went out to bingo, piling into dad's car for training – all good memories.

Yorkshire Pitmen's Champions

RUGBY LEAGUE

"The first man to kick a Rugby ball at Wembley."

Back in 1929 the Rugby League decided to take their showpiece 'The Challenge Cup Final' away from the Northern towns down to Wembley Stadium. It has since become a traditional pilgrimage for fans of this northern game. In the first ever final the honour of kicking off fell to Jim Rudd, a Featherstone man who was playing scrum half for Dewsbury against the mighty Wigan team.

We didn't get much in them days. About thirty bob for a win and you'd to play hard to get your place in the first team. We'd leave the pit Saturday morning and be stripped, ready to play a couple of hours later. Three nights a week training for no extra either.

I played my first Rugby for Sharlston Intermediates and then the George Street night school team in Featherstone. From there I was signed by Featherstone Rovers and made by debut at scrum half on Christmas Day 1923. It was a different game in them days, you'd have great big forwards, real hard men – you could have hit some of them with a shovel and they wouldn't have known about it. Then there were the speed men; centres like Jack Hirst, Harold Wagstaffe, nicknamed 'The Prince of Centres' and George Whittaker, who could run the length of the field in even time and hypnotise tacklers. That's what they did – hypnotise. They'd come at you swaying their hips one way and then another. Then you'd start going with them, moving from one side to another without wanting to and before you knew it, you'd be completely turned round and they'd passed and scored before you'd time to unknot your legs – marvellous!.

And the characters – I could talk all day. There was a referee who was a vicar, the Reverend Frank Chambers. He sent more men off the field than all the others put together.

If the Reverend was refereeing when Jonah Baggot was playing, you could bet your bottom dollar that Jonah wouldn't last the whole game. Mind you, Jonah was a big rough 'un, not frightened to get stuck in if there was any boot or fist to go in. Anyway, if you got *the early bath,* you got the cleanest water.

Considering they were hard men though, they'd hearts of gold. Matches were played for distress funds in aid of striking miners and we used to play regular matches for the local hospitals. Rovers played Castleford for Alderman Lyon's Cup for the benefit of Pontefract dispensary, and against Wakefield in aid of Clayton hospital. There was no National Health Service then.

They weren't easy games either, the lads took a lot of pride in those charity matches and they were very keen. I remember Jonty Parkin the famous tour captain coming to watch one of the games when I'd played well at scrum half.

"Where do Featherstone dig all these half-backs up from?" he wanted to know.

In the 1927/28 season, Featherstone Rovers surprised everybody except themselves when they reached the Championship Final. We played at Leeds in the semi-final and won when Sid Denton scored a glorious try. He picked it up at full back and ran the full length of the field. By hell it was a sight to see, a marvellous run. They were jumping like beans and there was some ale supped that night.

In the Final we played Swinton at Oldham. All the supporters were wearing wax babies on their coats because everybody knew Featherstone as 'The Babes' at that time. A lot of them had set off the night before to walk to Oldham because they couldn't afford the train fare. We couldn't manage it on the day though, Swinton was a fine team with the biggest pack of *forrads* about. They beat us eleven – nil. Mind you they'd won everything else that year so there was no shame in it.

I was transferred to Dewsbury at the end of that year, *policy of desperation* Featherstone called it – meaning they'd no money.

Lucky enough as it turned out for me, we managed to reach the Challenge Cup final in my first season there, with the added bonus that it was the first one to be staged at Wembley. The Rugby League Officials knew a lot of eyes would be on us and so they wanted an exciting spectacle – an open, fast game. That's what they call *attractive* football and they told us they wanted that type of game even before we got down to London. But that wasn't Dewsbury's style. They'd got where they were with dour football, hard tackling, straight up the middle stuff: whereas Wigan were used to open Rugby – faster men, you see. You could say that Wigan was bound to win before a ball was kicked.

Anyhow, we obeyed the League's instructions and tried to throw it about, but we just couldn't compete with Wigan in that style. They had some real speed merchants including Kinnear (he was the father of Roy Kinnear, the television comic.) We ended up losing 13 – 2, but I suppose I had the best honour of the day when I kicked off. At that time I didn't think about it, I'd always been a kicker and so naturally I was bound to land the job. I couldn't half kick, in fact I can still kick one today even at my age.

I stopped at Dewsbury till 1933 and ended up playing Junior Rugby till I retired. I've played whole games with a broken collar bone, played alongside the greats like Jack Hirst and company – I even played against Wigan in the Cup again. This time for Askern Juniors; I don't think I need to say who won that!

In 1979, when they had the Golden Jubilee celebrations down at Wembley, the survivors from both teams of 1929 were invited as guests of honour. I went and a few others did – but there's not many of us left now. It brought back a few memories though, I suppose it was my best day when I kicked off at Wembley.

WOMEN'S RUGBY

"For coppers in a bucket!"

Long before the women's soccer revolution in the sixties, women's cricket and the women's marathon; as long ago as 1919, the women of Featherstone organised a Rugby League team to support their striking menfolk. Mrs Alice Brear talks about the team's origins.

We first tried to start a Rugby team just after the Great War, when there was a pit strike on. We organised a game up at the Rovers' field but it ended with men complaining so we had to play soccer instead. Then in 1921, when there was another strike, we decided it was Rugby or nothing, ignored what the men had to say about it and went ahead. It was Mrs Williams who set it off, a big woman who lived in Mashams Square. There were lasses from all over though. I played at prop forward and a woman from Pontefract was the goal kicker. She could kick as well as any man and she'd only one eye.

Edi Asquith from the butcher's gave a leg of pork for the best player and there were tea and buns after the game.

Well, you should have seen us! We used to get changed upstairs in the Junction. We had to use the Rovers' kit and boots and then walk down to the ground. Billy Baltenwas our trainer and we went as 'Billy Balten's Thirteen'.

We had a woman referee – and scores of men came to watch. I think the men enjoyed it after a while, although they made fun of us a bit and we didn't like bending down in front of them to scrum off – but they couldn't do anything to stop us.

We played all over during that strike; Sharlston, Castleford, Ponte. They'd take up a collection for us, going round with a bucket, put on hot soup and buns for the strikers and dish out raffle tickets.

It was a good thing while it lasted but it had its drawbacks. I used to have to leave the young 'uns with a woman down the street and she fed them up till I came back — but you can't carry on like that. The other thing was, having to walk home in your muck and fill the tin bath for a wash.

We did it all again during the 1926 strike but there wasn't much call for womens Rugby after that.

Featherstone Ladies' Rugby Team raising money for the distress fund — ***1921***

Alpine Cyclo-cross

CYCLING

"A good vehicle for observation!"

Jim Travis got his first bike from East Hardwick Tip — "I couldn't afford to buy one of course." He became a member of Featherstone Road Club during the last war and continues his association with the club to the present day. He is also Chairman of 'The Bygone Bykes Yorkshire Club,' which boasts members as far afield as Australia and is said to be the main club in this country — north of the Wash.

Without a doubt, the bicycle is the finest mechanical device yet invented. It affords maximum enjoyment from physical endeavour — like walking or running with levers and you can go much further. It is also a good vehicle for observation.

The great days of cycling in this area were the 1930's, when many took to wheels in search of work, but biking for pleasure round here goes back much further. Old Featherstone Cycling Club was organising events as far back as the 1890's on tubeless tyres and they were racing on penny farthings at Headingley Cricket fields even before then.

Featherstone Road Club was formed in 1929 as a racing and touring club and we did have some good tours. There are a lot round here with fond memories of trips during the thirties to Springetts Tea Rooms, at Naburn near York. What a day out that was.

Of course, there were many other clubs. Every town had them, and in Featherstone alone I can name several. There was Purston C.C. which formed during the war and encouraged the reformation of the Featherstone Road Club which had lost many of its members to the services. Then there was Purston and Featherstone Wheelers, whose members were in it purely for pleasure. They'd no interest in racing and earned themselves the nickname 'The

Loiterers', a title they saw as derogatory, but one which summed them up fairly in the opinion of many. 'The Loiterers' had their meetings at the Jubilee Hotel – pubs were popular as meeting places for cyclists. Then there was the Jarvis family of Post Office Road, they had their own cycling club, made up just of Jarvis family members. It was a proper club too and registered as such with the National Cyclists Union.

Going back to the halcyon days though, the thirties saw a great deal of cycling activity and a lot of fun. A lot of it started when they shut down Featherstone Main Pit, and what with redundancies at other pits – a lot of men were left idle. Talk about *Get on yer bike,* well a lot of them did just that. The Copper Works at Leeds became big employers and seeing as nobody could afford the bus fares, everybody took to bikes. A convoy of them travelled from round here. Naturally, you'd get them racing each other, sprinting down Oulton straight, and round the bends at Methley, much the same as car drivers today. Out of this was spawned weekend pleasure trips and of course organised race meetings.

The majority of these racing events were illegal *flapper meets* on quarter mile tracks marked out with lime. There was big money to be made and when money is scarce, people will go to some lengths to obtain a share. They'd bet on themselves, on each other and most else that moved. There were some real harum-scarum boys as well; it didn't hurt too much falling off on grass and you'd get lads that were quite prepared to take a tumble in order to share in the proceeds. By a carefully designed fall you see, you could put your mates in the clear by taking out the other riders. *It's thy turn for a tumble* being a popular whispered invitation before many a race.

Betting went on illegally on many sports, cycling was no exception and a fair amount of brass changed hands up at Featherstone Welfare Cricket Fields, on the fields opposite the Jubilee and even on races at Rovers' Rugby ground.

Of course, the ultimate aim for a racing cyclist was to gain sponsorship from one of the manufacturers – few succeeded. The majority had to make do and mend, as they say. Riders for the Rudge Company, who had success with motorbikes at the Isle of

Featherstone Cycling Club on a day out

Man T.T. races, got their bikes for nothing. Then there was B.S.A. – that was the Birmingham Small Arms Company who developed round shot for killing folk during war time and then adapted the same shot as ball bearings for their bicycles during more peaceable times.

Featherstone Road Club reformed towards the end of the war and set up its headquarters in the St John's Ambulance Hut near Featherstone Railway station. Abraham Bullock, owner of the local bus company, put up a bit of money toward doing the place up and thus started the next great era of local cycling.

Emerging from the war years, Featherstone R.C. entered the fifties as a very ambitious organisation. They had smart maroon, blue and white racing colours and their own magazine *The Alpine Echo* – alpine referring to the spoil heaps or muckstacks around which the Cyclo-cross races were held. The club was able to put out a highly successful grass track, time trial and hill climb team and became highly respected organisers of many national events. The Cyclo-cross became immensely popular and in 1963, the Featherstone Club organised the only selection race for the World Championship. The course ran round the perimeter of the local colliery slag heaps starting with a 'Le Mans' type rush at Snydale. The bikes were placed about one hundred yards from the riders and at the gun there was a race to mount – a tricky business in itself because most cyclists are poor runners. Anyhow, the race was a huge success and was won by Keith Mernickle of the Middlesex Clarion Club. Keith later went on to further success on his shocking pink bike and was sponsored by the jazz musician Chris Barber, a keen cycling fan.

We went from strength to strength at this time and amongst other achievements we promoted and organised the first Cyclo-cross Professional Championship and arranged schoolboy and junior events.

Nowadays, the Featherstone club has members from all over the district and still promotes road racing and time trials. It also runs the only local time trial over hills, which is a thirty mile race in the Went Valley. This has taken place for over thirty years.

Of course, the competitions are one side, but much pleasure is still to be gained out of riding for the hell of it. Though the days are sadly gone when Pollard's bike shop in Station Lane advertised with the slogan *Sign on the dotted line and ride away singing till we meet again*. In fact there used to be three bicycle shops in one street in Featherstone – imagine that in a little town like this. It was easy then – a shilling a week on the never never, singing as you go. A bob a week on the finest mechanical device ever invented and one that's never been bested.

Featherstone Cricket Club – 1929/30

Featherstone and Purston Cricket Club, semi-finalists of Yorkshire Council – 1943

CRICKET

"Herbert Sutcliffe played for Featherstone"

While Rugby League remains ever popular in this area, the gentler summer pursuit of cricket runs a close second. George Johnson was involved with both games and tells about the burgeoning of the game in Featherstone from the beginning of the century until the end of the last war.

I suppose I'd be about six or seven years old when me and my mates used to go up to the cricket fields and lark about. We used to reckon to be cricketers and when we got fed up, we'd run about the delapidated pavillion and bars which hadn't been used since the outbreak of the first war. I remember there were old beer bottles strewn about everywhere. Ian Hague Beer, or *Iron* as they called it. 'Iron' Hague was the fearsome boxing champion from Mexborough who'd fought in America for the world title. Some said he was the world *fish and chip eating champion* as well.

There was a caretaker up at the ground, an ex-bobby who everybody was frightened of. 'Red Mick' they called him. I think it was less to do with his politics and more the colour of his face – he used to chase us all over the place.

The club reformed in 1919 as a Private Members Club funded by members' subscriptions and fund raising events. It had new headquarters at the Junction Hotel and a new name, 'The Featherstone and Purston Cricket Club'. There was a great period of activity during the following years and tennis and bowling sections were added during the early 1920's. Soon the name of Featherstone was one to be reckoned with in the cricket world.

But let me put it all into perspective and tell you a bit about the roots of the game round here. You see cricket was played in the district as far back as the 1860's when Purston Young Men's Association decided to form a cricket section. They were a lively lot and were well known for their debating society amongst other things. They had upwards of fifty members and in between cricket practice, they got together for debates with topics ranging from *the proposed Channel Tunnel* to a paper on *the meaning of dreams*.

The most important development came in the early 1900's with the formation of Featherstone Main CC. The club had headquarters at the Assembly Rooms, also known as the Miners Welfare or *Penny Slot*. It was funded by the colliery owner Colonel Shaw, but mainly by the miners at the pit who were stopped a few pence each week from their wages. Fields were obtained in North Featherstone and turf was specially imported from Cumberland – they said it was the finest in England at the time.

The club rapidly rose to prominence and became a top side in the county – partly due to the closure of a soap works in Wakefield. The story goes that Lever Brothers of Port Sunlight bought the Hodgson and Simpson soapworks and immediately closed down the Wakefield operation throwing many men out of work. The soap factory cricket team had been a very good one and top players from that side were offered employment at the Main, thereby making them eligible for the Colliery cricket side. Colonel Shaw, a canny old devil captured many county players in this way including Joe Denton, Harry Hartington and Jack Higgins, understudy to county keeper Art Dolphin.

Perhaps the biggest coup came when Herbert Sutcliffe, one of the finest English cricketers ever, was pursuaded to take a job in the colliery stores. With Ernest Moss, a demon fast bowler, Jackie Bedford, *the best uncapped player in the north* and the redoubtable Joe Bradbury, the Featherstone Club laid claim to the title, *Best Club Side in England*.

As you can see, the new club which formed from the ashes of the old one had a lot to live up to, but they set about their task with relish. Local tradesmen rallied round to provide much needed finance and a powerful ladies committee did some tremendous back up work. The Tennis and Bowling Sections also came into their own at this time and people actually queued up for the chance of a game.

One of the best events was the Sports Day held each year. Lord Masham would come and the gala was attended by thousands of local folk. There was cricket for charity as well as cycling – the Dixons and Millards would race, and athletic events with professionals like Fred Gill. Then the Ladies Committee put on *The Dance of the Year* at the Lister Baths – and what a night that was. The Rovers also held a Cricket Dance on New Year's Eve and a Rugby do on Boxing Day.

So where do I fit into all this? Well, I started with Featherstone Cricket quite by chance. I'd played about up at the field as a kid and then properly as a player for the King's School, but my big opportunity came during the great strike of 1926. I was thirteen at the time and standing at Cressey's corner to see the Tradesmen team off to a game in Leeds. They were a player short, so dad turned to me and said, "Go and get thee jacket and get on t'bus." And that was that. I played that day and made my debut for the first team the following season. I was a regular from then until the war intervened again.

Great Days! You see the Cricket Club was same as the Rugby Club, a community team. Everybody got on, at least most of the time. Although again like the Rugby club there were the same pitfalls. Some of the better players were enticed away by the professional clubs, others forsook cricket for other sports. At Rugby or soccer you see, the game finished at five and you'd be home for tea. At cricket the game might not finish till dark.

Finance was a constant worry. Everybody bought their own boots and whites and a decent bat cost anything up to two guineas (although you got one free if you topped the averages.) Bullocks bus cost £3 a trip, so to cut travelling costs, after the war I took half the team in my car. It was a *shooting brake* Ford V8. A lovely car, export model – we could get seven or eight into that.

For all the struggle, it was a happy club. Some *took the huff* after arguments, but they always came back. And laughs – we had some great times!

Once in training, I remember a good laugh at the expense of Toby Mason. After cricket we'd always have half an hour of Rugby. Toby was one for that. He'd be the one to shout, "Come on, let's get teams up." Anyhow, we'd been playing a bit when someone shouts, "There's an hedgehog in this hedge bottom!" Toby went running across to see it, tripped up on the long grass and fell flat on his face straight on the hedgehog. Well he came up cursing and swearing at the top of his voice and with a face redder than 'Red Micks'. We'd to pack up then. We couldn't carry on for laughing.

We had some fun with umpires as well. In a game at Bently the shout goes up, "HOWZAT??"

Umpire (lifting his finger) "OUT!"

Player, "Nay me leg wer noweer near."

Umpire, "I said OUT!"

Player, "Nay sir it wer never......"

Umpire, "Tha's bin in long enough – get on thi way."

Another umpire was Mr Hirst. He had a yeast round and sold yeast door to door to folk who made their own bread. Imagine that – making a living out of umpiring cricket and selling yeast.

Then there was the time at East Ardsley when the game ended in uproar. Fights started and bats were waved after Les Mason was judged out. He'd given the ball a real whack and thinking it had gone to the boundary, strode out of his crease to tap down a divot. The ball was returned and he was run out. This was most ungentlemanly conduct – just not cricket, as they say. Mind you, there were a few ungentlemanly players about at that time!

When the second war intervened, a lot of players were called up, including me. The club decided to carry on though. Bell and Killear, two of our players, were soon reported *killed in action* and when the great spin bowler Hedley Verrity of Yorkshire was also killed, the county selectors came to Featherstone in search of a replacement. They found their man in Arthur Booth, the slow left armer who was recalled to the Yorkshire side at the age of forty-three. He had a brilliant season and topped both the county and national averages in that same year with 111 wickets at 11.66.

Arthur went on to play professionally for several clubs in the Lancashire league.

In 1943, under the guidance of John Bramley, Featherstone were semi-finalists in the Yorkshire Council. In 1946 the club went one better and reached the final. In the semis, we beat the very strong Hickleton Club from Thurnscoe who could boast several country players including the Derbyshire men, Green and Tom Mitchell. We went down to Hanging Heaton in the final, a very professional outfit with rich backers.

I look back on the years between the wars with fond memories. A little community club with big ideas, no money but loads of talent. Boiling our own whites in coppers or set pots and relying on wives to make sandwiches and cakes.

When A.S. Dobson, the well known Rugby referee joined the club, he liked everything *just so* and organised new caps. Smart caps they were too, with rings round in Oxford and Cambridge shades of blue. Imagine that – Featherstone cricketers trotting onto the field in University blue.

Nora Carlile in goal – Yorkshire v. Lancashire tournament at St Anne's

HOCKEY

"A Cold Tap By The Bowling Green!"

Nora Carlile has played hockey since her schooldays and has been a long serving member to the Pontefract Club and to Yorkshire. Now at the 'experienced veteran' stage of her career she still gets the same thrill from playing as she did at school.

When I first joined Pontefract Ladies' Hockey Club, we played on a pitch in Pontefract Park over near the race course. During the week cows were allowed to wander onto the pitch, so you can imagine what state the pitch was in on a Saturday morning when we came to play. Beside this hazard, there were pot holes in the pitch and at times the ball completely disappeared down a hole. Then the game had to be held up while the ball was retrieved and put back on level ground.

Our changing facilities have improved tremendously over the years. Our first changing room was 'The Sons of Rest' pavilion, adjoining the bowling green in Pontefract Park. The windows had been smashed so often they'd been boarded up. The room was lit by a single bulb hanging from a wire leading from the men's changing room. We had no means of turning on this light – the switch was also in the men's room. As often happened, we finished our game before the men finished their soccer match and we had to wait until they came back before we could have any light in our place. The room was heated – but only just! Standing in the middle of the floor was a coal fired stove with its stove pipe leading up and out through the roof. The only snag was that the whole system was broken and cracked. Flames came out of the holes in the stove and the hot coals sometimes fell out. You had to keep your distance. Smoke often poured out so that we'd have to move out until the room cleared a little. Washing facilities were a bit primitive to say the least – a cold tap alongside the bowling green.

The facilities since have varied – sometimes we changed in people's front rooms. Imagine the mud and damp on the best carpet. We've used Pontefract High School changing rooms which were very pricey, Pontefract Cricket Club pavilion (for which we were very grateful), and Pontefract Rugby Club (entrance through the boiler house with its fumes). There was a shuttle service from there to the park and eventually to Featherstone Sports Centre. It seemed like heaven to us older members who had survived all the others.

Our home pitches have also varied considerably. At first, as mentioned, we played near the race course. We thought it was wonderful when we eventually got permission to play on the High School pitches. These were not in such good condition as the public tended to use themn for playing about on. Sometimes, we would have to clear youngsters off the pitch and they weren't very thrilled at having their games of soccer or what have you stopped. We'd occasionally have to fix up make shift goal posts when they'd been broken or sometimes removed completely. We also had to keep an eye open for golf balls zooming across the pitch (especially if anyone happened to slice it badly at the 2nd hole on the municipal course.) Now we use the *all weather* pitch at the Sports Centre – quite an improvement on the others.

Nowadays, we almost always travel by car to our matches, but not so in the past. We had to use public transport. Imagine getting across the centre of Leeds and changing buses on a busy, crowded Saturday lunchtime. It wasn't just us either, wherever we went babies came too. It was quite a sight. Picture the scene. Two people with a baby in carrycot between them and in their other hands, hockey bags with curved ends of hockey sticks sticking out, catching everything possible. No wonder we weren't very popular with shoppers when we crowded onto the buses.

Later, I progressed to a Lambretta motor scooter. At the time myself and another club member played for the Yorkshire County Team. Naturally, we had to travel greater distances for our matches – a home match might be at Hull, Sheffield, Ben Rhydding or Thirsk – and then there were away games. Our best means of getting to these matches or to a point where we could get a lift was my scooter. With our bags, sticks and my goal keeping pads strapped tightly to the bike's carrier, our mode of transport caused quite a lot of consternation and worry. But we never let anybody down and always arrived in good time, though there were sighs of relief when we eventually arrived at our destination.

When we played for the County Team, we used to spend the New Year at a Northern Counties tournament at St Annes near Blackpool. Over Christmas, we had to watch what we ate – not putting on too much weight or getting unfit. We often had to travel over to St Anne's on Boxing Day, which cut short any celebrations and then play a match a day for the next five days. Even New Year's Eve had to be a relatively sober affair as the teams generally played the next morning. This tournament was a very competitive affair. It decided which County Team would be Northern Champions – *Cock o't' North* for that season. Also at the end of the tournament *The North* team, comprising the best players from each county was announced.

On these away trips, I became renowned for my ability to sleep through anything. One occasion, after one of our team had been hit in the eye with a ball, an impromptu knock-about was arranged in my room to see if she could see the ball through the swelling. She couldn't and wasn't able to play next day. Another time a team mate who was rooming on her own, fell ill. She and my room mate dragged her bed into our room and she then fumbled about putting on a track suit because she was so cold. I didn't hear a thing and slept through both these events knowing nothing till next morning.

I well remember our first trip abroad – not counting a couple of trips to Ireland. The Yorkshire team had been invited to a hockey festival in Germany. On the Thursday before Whitsuntide I dashed home from work and caught the train to Sheffield. There I joined up with two other players and we drove to Watford where we stayedat another player's house. We spent most of the night chattering and after just a few hours sleep, were off bright and early to catch the 9 a.m. ferry from Dover. So far so good.

Once settled on board we wandered around looking for the rest of the team. Eventually we found one group – but one member was sitting muffled up in anorak and cagoul. We soon found out what was wrong with her....German measles. Another car load didn't make the ferry after breaking down – we just had to hope they'd arrive in time for our games. Then after docking, we faced another long drive – and only two of us could drive.

We'd been travelling over 20 hours when we finally arrived in the early hours of the morning. We were shown to our hotel rooms and I went straight to bed. In the middle of the night I began to feel sick and went to the bathroom. I remember putting my hand on the bathroom door handle – then I heard a great crash. The next thing I knew, someone was wiping my face with a wet cloth saying, "Come on. Wake up, wake up!" On hearing the crash, my room mate had jumped up shouting,' 'Someone's breaking in." She saw my empty bed, came into the corridor and there I was lying in a pool of blood – and blood spattered over the walls and everywhere. It seems I must have fainted, fallen back through a glass door, managed to crawl out and collapsed in the corridor.

Three team mates tried to get help from the hotel manager but none could speak German – he thought they were drunk. When they finally managed to get him to come up and see what had happened, he rang for an ambulance. Meanwhile, I was sitting on the floor flexing a badly cut thumb saying, "I can move it, I'll be okay to play tomorrow." But I wasn't. I had a long deep cut about 5' long down my arm and a very bad gash in the back of my thigh that you could fit your hand into! I had to have 27 stitches in all and was detained in hospital.

Imagine being stuck in a foreign hospital and not knowing the language. Luckily, the night nurse spoke Spanish and I'd been doing Spanish at night school so we managed a conversation of sorts, but I really looked foward to visits from my team mates.

After a few days, arrangements were made for me to be flown home along with two players from a men's hockey team from

Surrey, who'd also been at the festival. And what style I travelled home in! We arrived at Frankfurt Airport where I was provided with a wheelchair. I was wheeled to the Pan Am private lounge and after a few words, we were allowed entry. What a surprise! Deep pile carpets on the floor, plush seats, soft background music we could even sit down we were offered drinks and snacks. A stool was provided for me to rest my injured leg and a hostess kept coming to check whether I was comfortable or needed anything. This private lounge is apparently for those passengers who average 10,000 miles per year with Pan Am.

Another wheelchair was provided when I needed to board. I was lifted into the plane and was able to sit with my leg outstretched. On arrival in London, a limousine met the plane and I was transported to the terminal in it where another wheelchair was provided.

Later, I heard that the car in which I'd travelled to Germany, was involved in an accident on the way home and the car that had broken down on the way there also struggled to get back. It was decided that this trip was best forgotten in many ways. What a disaster! And I didn't even get to see the hockey fields!

Over the years, Pontefract have had their share of success. We have had members who have played for Yorkshire and The North at various levels and even an international player – all local girls.

For a few years we had some good results and were classed as one of the top four sides in the country. We won a variety of tournaments. Our indoor squad were in the National Finals at Crystal Palace on more than one occasion and again we had country players. Sadly, most of the team has grown old together and the legs and lungs are wearing out. A comment overheard in a refreshment tent recently went something like.... "Who's in the semi-final then?" "So and so, so and so, so and so and Pontefract." "What Pontefract! They're a team of geriatrics."

Our average age was thirty-six at the time but we still managed to beat a few of the younger teams. We went one better at the Ben Rhydding seven-a-side tournament though, we did well with a team with an average age of thirty-nine! Come on, you young ones!

SPORT AND GAMBLING

"Betting on two flies climbing a wall!"

When three sociologists; Dennis, Henriques and Slaughter visited Featherstone area during the 1950's they spent a lot of time in Working Men's Clubs and concluded that gambling was one of the most popular sports in the district. According to most sources, it was one of the few things they got right, because people told them "owt bar t'truth." There is no denying however the strong connection between local sports and gambling. Ted Fletcher tells of the attractions of having a bet — the pleasures and regrets.

Where it is you see, when a miner has spent all week *down the hole,* he needs bit of recreation in his spare time. I've seen me get my wage on Friday, go straight into the Welfare and start carding or dominoing. Some weeks I'd come home flush, but a lot of times I'd be skint. It's only then that I'd realise.... all week down that bloody place, working for next to nothing to start with and then chucking it away on ale and bloody dominoes. Then the following week I'd forget about it and go back for more. It took me years to learn my lesson and by hell it was hard learned.

I remember going to Sharlston once with my father, just after the war it'd be. There was a big money, darts match in a pub there. I've never seen as much side betting, plus a £25 purse for the winner. My dad was a good player, and when he'd supped a few pints and said, "Right! Get your brass on me," — *daft as a brush* I did. It was a one match '1001 up'. Every time he went on to oche, I bit my lip. Then he lost — with both of them on a double. £25 was a lot of money in them days, more than two weeks wages to a pitman.

It's always gone on round here though. I remember the older end always talked about a rugby match between Featherstone

Rovers and The Miners Welfare – it was the first time a big game had been played between two clubs from here. Everybody in Featherstone must have been there. Charlie Peel the referee, went mad when he saw what they were doing. He reported both teams and the crowd to the Rugby League Authorities saying that there were riots and hundreds of pounds were bet. Mind you, he must have exaggerated a bit, because there wouldn't be hundred pounds in Featherstone in them days.

It wasn't just rugby though. There was cycling and swimming and running, all of them popular with the gamblers. The favourite though was boxing. It was illegally arranged to start with, at the back of a pub or somewhere like that. Good hard fights with money to be made all round. Sometimes they'd even do it in the street – strip down to the waist and set to.

The Bobbies kept their eyes on us, but we normally got away. They used to play Bingo and Lotto Sunday afternoons on street corners, and post look-outs at either end. Then at Sharlston Common we had *tossing schools,* that was a gang who came to play pitch n'toss and other games with coins. There used to be some real bother at them do's – fighting between the players, Bobbies charging up over the common – and we used to run like hell.

All betting was illegal so you'd to be on your guard all the time. It wasn't too bad in the Clubs and Billiard Halls though. Up at The Palace snooker place in Station Lane they had about sixteen tables, you could get on for tuppence a game and stop on all day if you kept winning. Upstairs they had like a skittles game. It was a normal snooker table with a set of pins up at one end and you rolled a wooden ball at them. I've seen some crowds round that and plenty of money.

In the clubs, they used to put notices up:

Bagatelle, Cribbage, Dominoes.
Not to be played for money.

They still do today, nobody takes any notice though. That's the thing with gambling you see, its easy with so many turning a blind eye.

Horse racing didn't come popular till later. At one time you could only get a bet on legally at the course, but that didn't stop them setting up illegal betting offices, with a wireless and telephone link. They could afford to run the risk because they made enough money to easily pay the fine. There's no such thing as a poor bookie.

I remember a gang of my grandad's mates going to the horse racing at York in Ebor week. He couldn't go because he'd got skint playing *shoot* in the Club the night before so he sat at home brooding. Anyhow, he had last laugh. While they were gone he was rooting round the bins and found an empty salmon tin. As his mates were coming home down the backs, having got skint at York, he walks out with this empty tin on the flat of his hand, wiping his chops with his hanky and smacking his lips, he chucked it into t'midden and says, "By hell, that were bloody grand." Imagine their reaction – "Well bloody hell fire, here's us without ha'penny between us and that bugger's having salmon for his tea."

When you hear folk saying "I'll bet tha can," or "I'll bet tha can't," – it comes from folk like them trying to make a bit of extra. There were blokes down the pit who'd pile girders on their shoulders for a bet and I've heard that at Wheldale, they played *peggy* down the pit bottom – imagine that, running and pacing out down there. Ossie Wilkes used to carry sacks of corn or coal on his back to Wakefield for bets and managed it. And there were a few blokes who'd run each other to Pontefract and back for money. Others might have a few bob on a game of Shove Ha'penny or handball or even quoits.

Anybody will tell you though. It's a mugs game. The bookie is the only winner. I've taken a few bob off him, but he's had more off me. I wish I'd every pound back that I've given him.

CHILDRENS GAMES

"All Join In!"

Perhaps from the competitive element of children's games, an enthusiasm for sport develops. These are the memories of 'ex-players'.

I used to like the physical contact games. At George Street School, we played *All across,* some called it *Bulldog.* The idea was to have one in the middle and the rest would line up down a wall. When somebody shouted *All across,* everybody had to run to the other wall and avoid being tackled. Anybody caught had to stop in the middle to help the catcher till everybody was *catched.* I've skinned my knees a few times at that game.

Of course, we played *Tig* and a game with a ball called *Kingy – Hot Rice* they called it in Wakefield. You had to throw the ball at each other and if it hit, then they were on. *King o' the Castle* was another good one. It was everybody for themselves at that one. You had to get to the top of a hill or banking and stop everybody else coming up by throwing them back down.

Then there was *kick out can,* like a sophisticated form of *hiddy* where those who had been captured could be liberated by kicking over a tin can placed at the mouth of a den. Another variation of that was *sticks* or *Pegs,* where a ball was chucked at three pieces of wood stood against a wall. Gable end walls played a big part in a lot of games.

For the real rough 'uns there was *murder ball.* Everybody running with a bundle of old rags strapped up trying to rip each others clothes off. Sometimes we'd just race each other with nettles trying to sting their legs – short trousers in them days. Bravado games as well like *Midden jumping* – to see who could leap between most bin holes. Or swinging on wooden swings to get it *ont'locker* – that's to say make it go round a full 360 degrees. We used to torture those that wouldn't take part. Put them through the mill, everybody chanting and beating their backs with fists. Or we'd give them *Chinese burns* – blister their arms by rubbing the skin. If they were lucky, we might let them off lightly by just throwing 'sticky buds' onto their jumpers.

On the side of the Pit stacks at North Featherstone, they played the *Eton Wall Game.* Don't ask me how that came to Featherstone – but it was a proper game, they played it regularly. Mind you, I think they probably used a bit more violence than the lads at Eton will have done.

The older lads used to play *Peggy* or *Knurr and spell* as some called it. You got a tapered pick shaft and tapped up a small piece of wood that was placed on a brick. The idea then was to hit the small piece as far as possible. Bets would be taken then on how many strides it would take to pace it out.

At South Featherstone School, they played *stool board,* I think that game came from Suffolk. It was a bit similar to cricket, but the bat was like a wooden tennis racket and the wicket was a square board. South Featherstone School was where they used to chuck nippers over the rugby posts, then make them play at donkey battles, or *all pile on,* where everbody laid on top of each other – crushing the ones at the bottom.

*

At Love Lane School, the girls played mostly skipping games. I remember each one having its own chant. *Salt, Vinegar, Mustard, Pepper* was one of the most popular. We played hopscotch, whip n'top, everybody with her own pattern chalked on top. And *elastics,* that was a good game. Lengths of elastic stretched between the legs of two girls while another jumped in and out stretching the elastic into different patterns.

*

We had loads of games with tennis balls. Juggling against a wall accompanied by a rhyme, between two people, throwing against the kerb or at sticks.

I used to like it when the marbles season came round. All the squabbling and pushing and shoving round the *podges,* that's the holes the marbles went in to. There were all sorts of names for marbles as well; Nigs, Tors, Glass Alleys, and Bollys. My favourite marble game was *bobs along,* where you claimed your opponents Nig if you hit it by nudging yours toward it.

Jacks was a good game. They were like metal shapes that you caught on the back of your hand after tossing them in the air. If we'd any coppers we might toss them against a wall. The nearest one taking them all.

*

The most fascinating thing about children's games were the rituals and unwritten rules. It was as if the playground was some sort of magic place that opened up when the bell rang and closed again at the next ring. The words only kids know, like *Figgy* and *Laggy* and *Ranting.* Then we'd march round the playground with arms around each others shoulders chanting, "All join in if you're playing at......' – whatever the game was. Another way to start games was to form a ring, everybody legs apart while a ball was bounced in the middle. If the ball passed through your legs, you were on. Then there was the magic word. This was the word that temporarily excused you from being on. At George Street School, they said *Crosskeys,* elsewhere *Keys* and *Crosslegs* was used.

*

*

All up, all up,
Wherever you are.
If you don't want to play,
Stay where you are

Look at him, laugh at him,
Throw a lump of fat at him.

Ink, pink, pen and ink,
Who made that awful stink?
Out goes you.

A penn'orth of chips
To grease your lips
Out goes you!

What time is it Mr Wolf?
Dinner Time!

Jack, Jack, shine thee light.

Where was Moses when the light went out?
Down in the cellar wi' his shirt hanging out.

I draw a snake upon your back
Which finger did I draw it with?

Eeeni, Meeni, Macca, Racca.
Merr Rarr Dominacca
Chicka Bocka Lollipoppa
Rom Pom Push....... OUT!!

*

This book is one of a series of personal memories called *Speaking From Experience* – a number of people sharing a common experience telling their stories.

Other books in this series:
All in a Day's Work
Bathtime
In Sickness and in Health
Running for Clocks and Dessert Spoons

The Yorkshire Art Circus is a unique publisher. We link our books with performances, exhibitions and workshops. Our projects tour community centres, colleges, galleries, clubs, galas, libraries, schools and art centres, bringing new artists and writers to new audiences. For further details send for our brochure and booklist.